LONDON, NEW YORK, MUNICH, PARIS, MELBOURNE, AND DELHI

DESIGN • Jane Bull
TEXT • Penelope York
PHOTOGRAPHY • Andy Crawford
DESIGN ASSISTANCE • Laura Roberts
MANAGING EDITOR • Sue Leonard
MANAGING ART EDITOR • Cathy Chesson
PRODUCTION • Shivani Pandey
DTP DESIGNER • Almudena Díaz

For my cooking teacher Barbara Owen
(who's also my mother)

First American Edition 2002

01 02 03 04 05 10 9 8 7 6 5 4 3 2

Published in the United States by
DK Publishing, Inc.
375 Hudson Street
New York, NY10014

DK Publishing offers special discounts for bulk purchases for sales promotions or premiums. Specific, large-quantity needs can be met with speical editions, including personalised covers, excerpts of existing guides, and corporate imprints. For more information, contact Special Markets Departments, DK Publishing, Inc. 375 Hudson Street, New York, NY10014
Fax: 800-600-9098

Library of Congress Cataloging-in-Publication Data
Bull, Jane, 1957-
   The cooking book/by Jane Bull.--1st ed.
     p. cm.
   Summary: Illustrations and simple text provide instructions for creating a variety of foods.
   ISBN 0-7894-8834-5
     1. Cookery--Juvenile literature. [1. Cookery.] I. Title.

TX652.5 .B7476 2002
641.5'123--dc21

2002019499

ISBN: 0-7894-8834-5

Color reproduction by GRB Editrice S.r.l., Verona, Italy
Printed and bound in Italy by L.E.G.O.

see our complete product line at
www.dk.com

Stir up something tasty

The Cooking Book

Jane Bull

DK

A Dorling Kindersley Book

what's cooking in this book..?

Getting started 4-5

Your cooking kit 6-7

Play dough 8-9

How to make play dough 10-11

Popcorn 12-13

Pick and mix soup 14-15

Stir up some soup 16-17

delicious dishes and

Pasta 18-19

Fruity tarts and cheesy quiches   20-21

Roll out the fruity tarts 22-23

Moon rocks 24-25

Mission moon rock 26-27

Mix up a mud pie 28-29

Mixing the mud 30-31

tantalizing treats!

Rainbow cakes 32-33

Conjure up some colorful cupcakes 34-35

Upside-down cake 36-37

Turn a cake upside down 38-39

Cool fruit 40-41

How to make smooth fruit slurps 42-43

Pit-stop snacks 44-45

Cooking words 46-47

Index 48

Getting Started

Follow this advice before you begin, and you will find the recipes much easier and safer. But most important, ENJOY IT!

Safety first
Taking care in the kitchen

You should always tell an adult what you are doing in the kitchen so they can be around to help you.

⭐ warning star

Watch out! The kitchen can be a dangerous place unless you are careful and use tools properly. When you see this symbol it means that something is hot, sharp, or electric, or otherwise may need adult help.

It's hot!

⭐ Ask an Adult

When you see this sign it means that you need adult help.

Hot ovens and steaming pans

Always wear oven mitts when you are using the oven. Let hot food stand to cool, and beware of hot steam.

It's electric!

Electric tools

Make sure you have an adult with you when you are using electrical items. Your hands should be dry when you use them. Always unplug them when finished.

It's sharp!

Sharp knives

Watch your fingers when you slice and NEVER walk around carrying a knife.

Kitchen rules

It makes sense to keep a kitchen clean and tidy when you're cooking; so here are some tips.

Cover up Wear an apron or old shirt.

Wash up Scrub your hands clean.

Tidy up as you go along.

All set? Let's cook!

Measuring

Set out your ingredients before you start so you don't leave anything out.

Measurements

Here are a few easy measurement conversions:

3 teaspoons = 1 tablespoon
2 tablespoons = 1 ounce
8 ounces = 1 cup

KITCHEN SCALES

A Spoonful

In this book a spoonful is flat on top, not rounded. Try using a measuring spoon, they have standard sizes from a tablespoon right down to $1/8$ teaspoon.

MEASURING CUP

MEASURING SPOONS

How Much will it make?

This symbol will tell you how much the recipe will make, for example, "makes 12 cakes."

How long will it take?

When you see this little clock symbol in a recipe, it tells how long the meal or snack will take to cook.

Food facts

Food is amazing stuff. It tastes good and is fun to play with, but best of all it keeps you alive. Your body needs different foods to keep you well and happy. Here are a few types.

Body builders

You can find proteins in meat, eggs, milk, cheese, fish, nuts, and beans. They help your body grow and make muscles strong.

Bug busters

Vitamin C found in fruit and vegetables, like oranges, broccoli, and potatoes helps your body fight off infections like colds and flu. You should eat at least five servings of fruit and vegetables a day.

Energy food

Carbohydrates, from foods like cereal, pasta, rice, and bread, give your body energy. So if you're running around or playing sport they will help you last longer.

Treats and sweets

Sugary foods that taste really good give you short bursts of energy that don't last very long. However even though candy, cake, and chocolates, taste good, it isn't healthy to eat too much of them.

I want to grow up big and strong

your cooking kit

Ask an adult to help with sharp knives

Fork   Spoons   Sharp knife   Wooden spoon   Spatula

Here are the tools used in this book

It's always best to gather all the tools you need before you start cooking.

Large mixing bowl

Small bowl

Big bowls

There is nothing more tricky than having to mix too much in a small bowl. Always choose one that can hold double your mixture.

Hand blender

Blender

Ask an adult to plug in the electrical gadgets

Electric tools

Electric tools help with all of those jobs that make your arm tired. But if you don't have them it's not the end of the world. You'll just have to mix by hand!

Electric mixer

6

Rolling pin

Pastry cutters

Sieve

Pastry brush

Cutting board

Small saucepan

Large saucepan with lid

⭐ Ask an adult to handle hot pans

8 in (20 cm) cake pan

8 in (20 cm) cake tin with removable bottom

Muffin pan and cupcake liners

Cookie sheet

Foil

Plastic wrap

Wire rack

Peeler

Play dough

Have fun with bread dough: Squeeze and shape it, watch it rise – then eat it hot from the oven.

To make your dough collect these ingredients

1 packet (7 g) easy blend yeast

1½ lb (750 g) unbleached flour

1½ cups (450 ml) warm water

1 teaspoon salt

2 teaspoons sunflower oil

Makes about 10 plain rolls

Shine up your shapes by brushing them with beaten egg

To decorate your dough

1 beaten egg

Sunflower seeds

Poppy seeds

Raisins

8

1. Mix it all up

Put the yeast, flour, warm water, salt, and oil into a bowl and mix them together.

2. Take the mixture out

Sprinkle the worktop with flour, and take the mixture out of the bowl.

3. Start kneading

To knead, press your fist hard into the dough, then turn the dough and do it

How to make play dough

Have some fun playing with your bread dough. You'll really love to squeeze it. Squish it around, roll it into shapes, then decorate it by making a whole bread family. Watch it rise, and when it's baked, serve it up hot with butter. Yum!

7. Place on a greased sheet

Make sure you place the shapes far apart from one another.

8. Leave them to rise

Cover the dough on the tray loosely with plastic wrap and leave in a warm place for 30 minutes until it doubles in size.

4. keep kneading
Knead for 10 minutes.
The dough should be stretchy, not sticky.

5. Cut up the dough
Divide the dough into smaller pieces
or pull off chunks to play with.

6. Play
Choose a design - try making faces.
Preheat the oven
to 425°F/220°C.

PLAY DOUGH TOOLS

MIXING BOWL

WOODEN SPOON

PASTRY BRUSH

PLASTICWRAP

KNIFE

BAKING TRAY

WIRE RACK

9. Brush on egg and decorate
Brush the bread with beaten egg and decorate with seeds or raisins.

11. Bake your bread
Bake for 10–15 minutes. The small shapes
will cook faster, so take them out sooner.

Popcorn ✱

Pop ✱ pop ✱ Pop ✱ Have a ✱Pop✱ at making Popcorn. But keep the Pop lid on, or it'll Pop everywhere!

Butter popcorn

1 tablespoon oil

1/4 cup popping corn

4 tablespoons butter

☺ Makes one big bowlful

Sweet or Salty

Sprinkle sugar or salt over popped popcorn while it is still in the pan.

TOOLS FOR ✱Pop✱ POPCORN

SAUCEPAN WITH LID

WOODEN SPOON

12

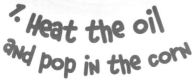

Let the oil get really hot.

*pop *pop

pop*

When the popping stops, give the pan a shake.

1. Heat the oil and pop in the corn

 Ask an adult to help with the very hot pan.

2. Pop on the lid and listen for pops

Cook for about a minute, or until there are no more pops. Use oven mitts if the pan is hot.

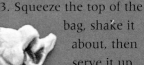 **Bags of flavor**

For some more exciting tastes to add to your butter popcorn:
1. Put your popcorn into a clean plastic bag.
2. Shake in grated cheese or dried herbs,
3. Squeeze the top of the bag, shake it about, then serve it up.

Take it off the burner to cool it down.

You won't need any heat under the pan.

3. Turn off the heat and take a peak

4. Stir in the butter, it's ready to eat

Pick and Mix Soup

Make up
Try making it green or orange,
smooth or chunky,
but most of

Cook this mix up for starters

 Makes about two big bowls or ten tiny ones

Pat of butter

Onion

Red pepper

Apple

Carrot

1 cup (600 ml) water

 Bouillon cube

 Mixed herbs

your OWN recipe
sweet or salty,
mild or spicy –
all, make it
tasty

what did the big MUG
say to the little MUG?

Eat up, and SOON
you'll be as big as me!

15

Stir up Some Soup

Chop Chop Chop

Get souped-up to make this yummy appetizer. All it takes is lots and lots of chopping. Cut the vegetables into small pieces, and the rest is simple.

No more tears if you chop the onions with goggles on

SOUPER TOOLS

CHOPPING BOARD

SHARP KNIFE

SPATULA

PEELER

LARGE SAUCEPAN WITH LID

GOGGLES

Ask an adult to help with sharp knives.

Chop off the top and the bottom, then pull off the skin

---

1. Melt the butter
in the saucepan over low heat.

2. Add the onions,
keeping the heat low so that they don't burn.

3. Cook slowly
for about a minute until the onions look see-through and soft.

4. Add the rest
the chopped apple, pepper, and carrot.

Slice, dice, and chop...

keep your fingertips tucked away

The smaller the pieces, the quicker the soup will cook.

and they're ready for the pot

Remove the seeds and core from the apple and pepper

A Smooth Soup

If you don't like lumpy soup, use a blender until it is smooth. **LET THE SOUP COOL** before you start blending.

Ask an adult to help you use a blender.

5. Pour in the water
herbs, and bouillon cube.

6. Let it boil
for a minute by turning up the heat.

Cook for 30 minutes.

7. Gently simmer
Turn the heat down and simmer for 30 minutes over a low heat.

Watch out, the steam is HOT!

Souper! It's ready to eat

8. Check the soup
Make sure everything is cooked.

Perfect pasta

1. Boil some water

Fill a pot about 2/3 full with water.
Bring to the boil, then add the pasta.

⭐ **Ask an adult** to help with the hot water

2. Cook the pasta

Boil for about 10 minutes
or follow instructions on the package.

3. Drain the water

Rest the sieve on the pan.
Now the pasta's ready to serve.

Tomato Sauce

1. Heat the oil

Peel and chop the garlic,
then fry it in the saucepan.

2. Add tomatoes

⭐ **Ask an adult** to help as the oil will get hot.

3. Let it simmer

Add the herbs and sugar and stir.
Let simmer for 2 minutes.

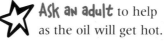

Choose your pasta

4 ounces (125 g) any quick cook pasta

Water

Tomato sauce

1 small can of chopped tomatoes

1 tablespoon olive oil

1 clove garlic

1 teaspoon sugar
1 teaspoon herbs

TOOLS FOR PASTA

2 SMALL SAUCEPANS FOR PASTA AND SAUCE

SIEVE OR COLANDER

SPATULA

Quick cook pasta

Try out all sorts of shapes and sizes

Pasta

cook up a quick meal

of pasta with a tasty tomato sauce

Dish up dinner

When the sauce is ready, spoon it over the pasta and stir it up. Chop up some fresh herbs, such as basil leaves, for decoration, and grate some cheese for extra taste.

Makes 2 helpings

flour
1 1/3 cups (175 g)

butter
1 tablespoon (90 g)

water
2 tablespoons

red jam
1/2 cup (125 g)

Fruity tarts and cheesy quiches

Sweet or Savory - these tarts can be both. A sweet after-school treat or a cheesy mini-meal. Pop them into your lunchbox as delicious snacks.

🥤 Short crust pastry

Once you know how to make this pastry, you'll find that you can make lots of dishes. You can make apple pies, quiches, and much more.

= fruity tart ×

Roll out the fruity tarts

When you make the short crust pastry, be sure that you don't put in too much water; add a little at a time. Succeed with your tarts and you can call yourself a professional pastry chef! Experiment with fillings and test them on your family.

FRUITY TART TOOLS

LARGE MIXING BOWL WIRE RACK MUFFIN PAN

SPOON 3 IN (7.5 CM) PASTRY CUTTER ROLLING PIN

Try these savory cheese quiches

You'll need

Short crust pastry, the same as the fruity tarts
2 eggs
$1/4$ cup (60 g) grated cheese (Cheddar is a good choice.)
$3/4$ cup (150 ml) milk

1. Prepare the pastry in the same way as for the fruity tarts.
2. Beat the eggs in a bowl. Add the grated cheese and milk.
3. Spoon the mixture into the pastry shells.
4. Bake them in the same way as the fruity tarts.

Top them off with half a cherry tomato

22

1. Mix together
the flour and butter with your fingers.

5. Make a ball of pastry
The bowl will be clean when it's ready.

9. Cut the shells
The left over pieces can be shaped and

2. Keep mixing
until the mixture looks like coarse breadcrumbs.

3. Add some water
Pour about two tablespoons into the mixture.

4. Squeeze it
Bring the mixture together into a ball.

6. Sprinkle flour
over the ball, rolling pin, and countertop.

☆ Preheat the oven to 400°F/200°C.

7. Press down the ball
Turn the pastry as you roll it. Add flour to the table if it sticks.

8. Start rolling
It should be about 1/8 in (4 mm) thick.

10. Spoon in the filling
Only half fill the shells with jam.

11. Bake the tarts
Bake in the oven for about 15 minutes. ☆

Royal tarts for the queen of hearts

Let them cool – if you can wait!

MOON rocks

YOUR MISSION – to make moon rocks
that are good enough to eat. Read the scientific
data carefully and report back at snacktime.

THIS IS WHAT MOON ROCKS ARE MADE OF

1 ¼ cup (250 g)
self rising flour

6 tablespoons (90 g)
soft brown sugar

6 tablespoons (90 g)
butter

½ cup (125 g)
raisins

One pinch
of salt.

½ teaspoon
pie spice

1 egg

Collect these
samples, then
turn the page
to receive your
instructions for
moon rock
construction

 Makes 8-12
moon rocks

One small step for man,
one giant heap
of cake for me!

24

Other space rocks to find

Leave out the raisins and try these other tasty rocks.

Comet cocktail
1/2 cup (125 g) chocolate chips

Meteor shower
1/2 cup (125 g) sugar strands

Mars attack
Add 1 teaspoon of red food coloring at the same time as the egg.

MISSION MOON ROCK

Collect your samples and prepare your work area. Check the tools and follow these instructions to proceed. Remember Captain, you must be back from a successful mission by snack time. Good luck.

MIXING BOWL

FORK

COOKIE SHEET

WIRE RACK

1. Throw in the butter and flour

Rub it between your fingers and thumbs until it looks like bread crumbs.

2. Add the sugar and raisins

Mix them up evenly using your hands. Add the pie spice, too.

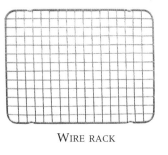

6. Grease th

Spread some butter over t

Preheat the ove
400°F/200°C.

3. Beat the egg in a separate bowl

Then add the beaten egg to the mixture.

4. Mix together with a fork

Make sure it's all mixed well.

5. Stick your hand in and squeeze

Gather all the bits in the bowl and squeeze them together into a ball.

8. Bake them ⭐

Bake in the oven for about 15 minutes.

Yummy! Accomplished mission Captain!

Let them cool on a rack.

Mix up a mud pie

Load 'em up! Move in the trucks to collect the materials for your mud pie. This is a mix that you don't even need to bake – IT'S SO EASY!

Chocolate sprinkles

1 chocolate bar for topping

1/2 cup (125 g) castor sugar

WARNING! Mud Pie under construction

1 tablespoon cocoa powder

3/4 cup (175 g) butter

1/2 cup (125 g) mixed dried fruit

1 cup (250 g) graham cracker crumbs

Drive up and drop on some chocolate sprinkles

Makes about
12 slices

Check out this slice

Mixing the mud

Shovel up all of the muddy ingredients in a saucepan, pack the earth down hard into the pan, pop into the fridge, and dump it out when it's ready. Add more mud and serve.

1. Melt the butter
★ Don't get it too hot, just melt it!

5. Line cake pan with foil

TOOLS TO MIX THE MUD

SAUCEPAN

KNIFE

WOODEN SPOON

8 INCH (20 CM) DIAMETER CAKE PAN

FOIL

Try these mini mud pies

Finish the mini-pies with grungy mud topping and worms or other gummy candy.

* Mix up the mud the same way as for the big pie.
* Put some paper cupcake liners in a muffin tin and divide the mud up equally.
* Place in the fridge to set.

wheel out those pies!
Vroom Yum

☺ Makes about 12 mini-pies

30

How to make the Muddy topping
* Pour some very hot water into a bowl and place another bowl on top of it.
* Break up the chocolate and place it in the top bowl.
* Let the heat melt it.

★ Ask an adult to help with the hot water.

2. Add cocoa and sugar
Take the pan off the heat to do this.

3. Now add fruit and graham cracker crumbs

4. Mix it all up

6. Pour in the Mix

7. Pr

The steam will melt the chocolate.

Put the bowl of chocolate on top of a bowl of hot water.

1. melt the chocolate

2. Pour it on

3. Spread it out

Rainbow cakes

Heaps of colorful rainbow cakes cover the party table. Bake cupcakes and decorate them as magically you can.

Conjure up Colorful Cupcakes

A measure, a whisk, and the swish of a wand.

1/2 cup (125 g) self rising flour

1/2 cup (125 g) butter (room temperature)

1/2 cup (125 g) castor sugar

1 teaspoon baking powder

2 eggs

1 teaspoon vanilla extract

 Makes 24 cupcakes

CUPCAKE UTENSILS

MIXING BOWL

TEASPOON

TABLESPOON

SIEVE

WIRE RACK

ELECTRIC MIXER

Fill them with paper cupcake liners.

2 MUFFIN PANS

Rainbow icing

 To ice 4 cakes

Mix up lots of little bowls of different colored icing. For green icing, mix yellow and blue; for orange, mix yellow and red. Use anything sweet to decorate the tops, such as glazed cherries, raisins, or sprinkles.

1 tablespoon confectioners' sugar

1 teaspoon water

1 drop food coloring

1. Mix the water, food coloring, and confectioners' sugar.

2. Drop a small dollop of icing into the center of the cupcake and let it spread.

3. Decorate the cupcakes with anything sweet, and use tubes of writing icing for extra patterns.

Sieving adds more air

1. Sieve the flour and baking powder

⭐ Set the oven to 375°F/190°C.

5. Fill up the liners

Put a teaspoon of mixture in each.

Bake in the oven for 20 minutes.

3. Beat until creamy

4. Does it drop off a spoon?
If it drops off easily in a dollop, then it's ready.

2. Add everything else
Beat the eggs and throw them in with the butter, sugar, and vanilla extract.

6. Take out of the oven
☆ Ask an adult to help with the hot oven.

Shhh... cupcakes cooling

upside-down

Looks like a plain, old cake, but turn it over for a fruity surprise!

1/2 cup (125 g) self rising flour

1/2 cup (125 g) butter

1/2 cup (125 g) sugar

2 beaten eggs

1 teaspoon vanilla extract

1 teaspoon baking powder

Hidden fruits to try: raisins, glazed cherries, canned mandarin oranges, peaches, pineapple, apricots

cake

Serve your cake hot and steaming with ice cream

Makes one big cake or 24 cupcakes.

Turn a cake upside down!

All you do is make the cake backward, starting with the top and ending with the bottom! For upside-down cupcakes, use a muffin pan with individual portions. Have fun doing it the wrong way around!

UPSIDE-DOWN TOOLS

ELECTRIC MIXER

LARGE MIXING BOWL

SIEVE

8 INCH (20 CM) DIAMETER CAKE TIN WITH REMOVABLE BASE

LARGE SPOON

KNIFE

SERVING PLATE

MUFFIN PAN FOR CUPCAKES

Sift the flour.

1. Put all the cake ingredients in a bowl

4. Arrange the fruit
Lay the pieces down so they will look their best when you flip the cake

8. Cover with a plate

9. Now flip it over
Using oven mits, put one hand on each side.

It's ready when it drops easily off the spoon in a dollop.

2. Beat until creamy

3. Grease the tin

⭐ Preheat the oven to 375°F/190°C.

cool fruit

Eat us just the way we are,

or mix us into smooth fruit cocktails
then freeze us for super-cool ice pops.

Banana and apple Slurp

1 banana
1 apple
1 1/2 cups (450 ml) milk
1 tablespoon yogurt
Prepare the fruit,
Blend and serve.
Sweeten to taste.

Strawberries and cream

1/2 cup (125 g) strawberries
1/2 cup (150 ml) milk
1/2 cup (150 ml) cream
Prepare the fruit,
blend, and serve.
Add extra sugar to
sweeten it up.

The big freeze
Very cool ice pops

Mix up your fruit drink, pour it into
molds, and pop them into the freezer.
Drink any leftover juice.

Kiwi

Grape

Banana

Strawberry

Apple

Five fruit cup
Just peel, chop up
and fill a cup for an instant snack.

Cream of kiwi

2 Kiwis
1 1/2 cups (450 ml) milk
Prepare the fruit,
blend, and serve.
Add sugar or honey
to sweeten.

How to make Smooth fruit Slurps

Try out different varieties of fruit

Fresh fruit is best if you can find it easily. If not, frozen or canned fruit and its juice is good, too. To prepare the fruit, remove the stalks and peel – you want to make your drink as smooth as possible, so the fewer bits the better.

☆ **Ask an adult** to help with the blender and the sharp knife.

To make a pink drink

Milk   Ice cream   Sugar

☺ Makes 2 smooth glasses

6 or 7 large strawberries
1 banana
$1/4$ cup (60 g) raspberries
$1^1/2$ cup (450 ml) milk
1 scoop ice cream
2 teaspoons sugar

1. Prepare the fruit ☆

2. Drop in the ☆ fruit

42

Inventing your own Slurp

There are so many ways to make your own original fruit smoothies – you just have to experiment. Try adding some of these ingredients to your fruit mixture. A good way to do it is to add a little at a time and keep tasting. If your drink isn't sweet enough, add a spoonful of sugar or honey.

Sugar or honey

Don't forget to squeeze me – I'm tangy

Lemon juice

Water of fruit juice

Milk or cream in small amounts

Ice cream

Plain or fruit yogurt

Now pour it out and slurp away ahh... delicious

3. Add the rest
Throw in the milk, ice cream, and sugar.

4. Screw the lid on tight
Blend for 40 seconds.

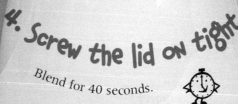

Healthy Snack cups

Vegetable sticks and your home-made breadsticks for dipping.

Plastic cups are perfect for all sorts of dips.

Mix some cream cheese and plain yogurt to your taste.

Mixed nuts and dried fruit make tasty tidbits.

Pit-Stop Snacks

Ready, Set, go!

Just like a race car, you need to fill up with fuel, too! Brrrrrooomm.

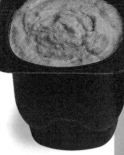

A candy car

With a quick power boost, I go well for a short distance.

Display the treats on a plate - but don't be tempted to eat them all yourself!

Try a wheel change

Chop up some fruit and arrange into pictures. Wheel in the vitamin C.

Sweet Snack cups

Mix together some cream cheese and fruit yogurt for a fruit dip.

Fill a cup to the brim with candy. Squeeze as many in as you can.

Pop your homemade popcorn into cups for a quick snack.

Cut fruit sticks and slices for dipping or eating on their own.

Dips and Snack cups

Pit stop snacks are perfect for parties or when you need to refuel. Fill up a cup and munch away! Eat as much of the fruit and vegetables as you like but put the brakes on when it comes to sweets!

weee... are full of energy!

A veggy racer

I'm the winner! The veggies beat the sweets!

Checkered flag Sandwich

For the beginning and end of the race, rustle up a tasty checkered flag. Take two pieces of bread, one white and one dark brown, and spread them with cream cheese. Place the white over the brown, and cut into squares. Arrange them as a flag.

Cooking words – greasing a pan
* rolling * creaming * slicing * beating eggs

Dough
This is the word for the thick, squishy flour mixture before it is cooked. It can be bread, cookie, or pastry dough.

Kneading
Bread dough has to be kneaded, or turned and squashed a lot, to help spread the yeast throughout the dough.

Rising dough
After kneading the dough, leave it to sit and rise for a while. This lets the yeast react, and the dough will grow to twice its size.

Boiling
This is when the heat is turned up high and the liquid in the pan bubbles busily. Mostly you only boil for a short time, then let it simmer.

Simmering
Once the liquid boils, you can turn the heat down and let it simmer. This means letting the liquid bubble gently and steadily.

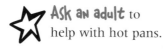
Ask an adult to help with hot pans.

Breaking an egg
First tap the side of the egg hard on the rim of a bowl. Dig both of your thumbs into the hole you have made and pull the shell apart. Remember, always wash your hands after handling eggs.

Beating eggs
Before adding eggs to ingredients, it's best to beat them first. Stir the eggs very fast with a fork.

* chopping * boiling * simmering * rubbing in
* sifting * kneading * rising

Here's a description of what they mean.

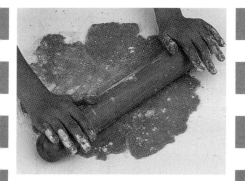

Rolling dough

Sprinkle flour on the countertop and rolling pin before you start rolling, and keep sprinkling throughout to deep the dough from sticking.

Chopping and Slicing

A recipe will tell you how big to chop or slice something. Always be careful when you use a knife.

★ **Ask an adult** to help with sharp knives.

Rubbing in

For cookie and pastry, the way to mix the flour and butter together is to rub them between your fingers and thumbs. Keep rubbing until the mixture looks like bread crumbs.

Greasing a pan

To deep food from sticking to a baking sheet, smear a little oil or butter all over the surface with your fingers. Get it right up to the edges.

Sifting

Sifting flour removes the lumps and adds air, which is good for making cakes. Gently tap the sieve against your hand to let it through.

Creaming

The cakes in this book use the one-stage method where the ingredients are all put together at the start. To cream, you blend this mixture until it falls off a spoon easily.

INDEX

Angelica 36
Apple 21, 41
Apricot 36
Apron 4

Baking powder 34, 36
Banana 41, 42
Biscuit 28, 31, 46, 47
Bread 5, 8, 10, 11, 45, 46
Breadstick 44

Cake 24, 33, 38, 47
Candy car 44
Carbohydrate 5
Cheese 5, 13, 19, 20, 22
Chocolate 5, 25, 28, 29, 30, 31
Cocoa 28, 31
Comet cocktail 25
Cool fruit 40-43
Cream 41, 43
Cream cheese 44, 45
Creepy-crawly 30

Dip 45
Dough 8, 10, 11, 46, 47

Fairy cake 33, 34
Five fruit cup 41

Flag sandwich 45
Flan 20
Food colouring 25, 34
Fruit cocktail 40
Fruit juice 43
Fruity tart 20-23

Garlic 18, 19
Glacé cherry 34, 36
Grape 41

Herbs 13, 14, 18, 19
Honey 41, 43
Hummus 44

Ice cream 37, 42, 43
Icing sugar 24

Jam 20

Kiwi fruit 5, 41
Knead 10, 11, 46

Lemon 5, 43
lolly 40

Mars attack 25
Meteor shower 25
Moon rocks 24-27
Motor car 44
Muddy topping 30-31
Mud pie 28-31

Nuts 44

Orange 5, 36
Oven mitts 4, 38

Party table 33
Pasta 5, 18-19
Pastry 21, 22, 46, 47
Peach 36
Pineapple 36
Pink drink 42
Pit-stop snacks 44-45
Popcorn 12-13, 45
Protein 5

Queen of hearts 23

Rainbow cakes, 32-35
Raisin 8, 24, 25, 26, 34, 36
Raspberry 42

Safety 4
Sandwich 45
Savoury snackpots 44
Seed 8, 11, 17
Slurp 41, 42
Smoothie 43
Snack 20, 44, 45
Soup 14-17
Spice 24, 26
Strawberry 41, 42
Sweets 5, 34, 44, 45

Tomato sauce 18, 19

Upside-down cake 36-39

Vanilla essence 34, 35, 36
Vitamin C 5, 40, 44

Writing icing 34

Yeast 8, 10, 46
Yogurt 41, 43, 44, 45

ACKNOWLEDGEMENTS

With thanks to . . .
Maisie Armah, Charlotte Bull, Billy
Bull, James Bull,
Jackelyn Hansard, and Josephine
Hansard for being model cooks

All images © Dorling Kindersley.
For further information see:
www.dkimages.com